THE STORY BEHIND
DIVING

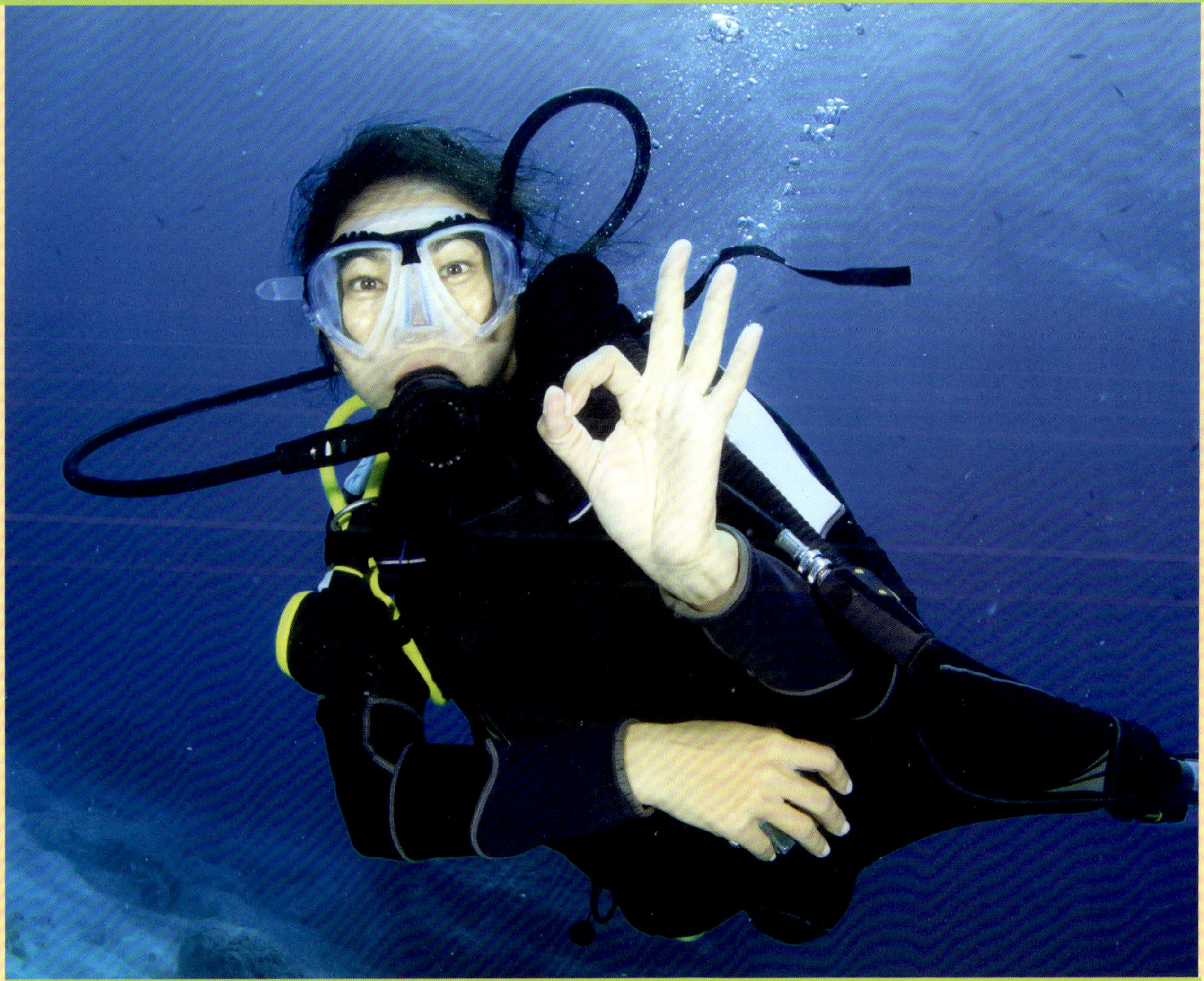

WRITTEN BY PAUL ROBINSON

CONTENTS

INTRODUCTION TO DIVING	4	UP CLOSE AND PERSONAL	12
CLIFF DIVING	6	SCUBA DIVING	14
NO PLACE FOR FEAR	8	SCUBA SIGHTS	16
CAGE DIVING	10	BLUE HOLES	18

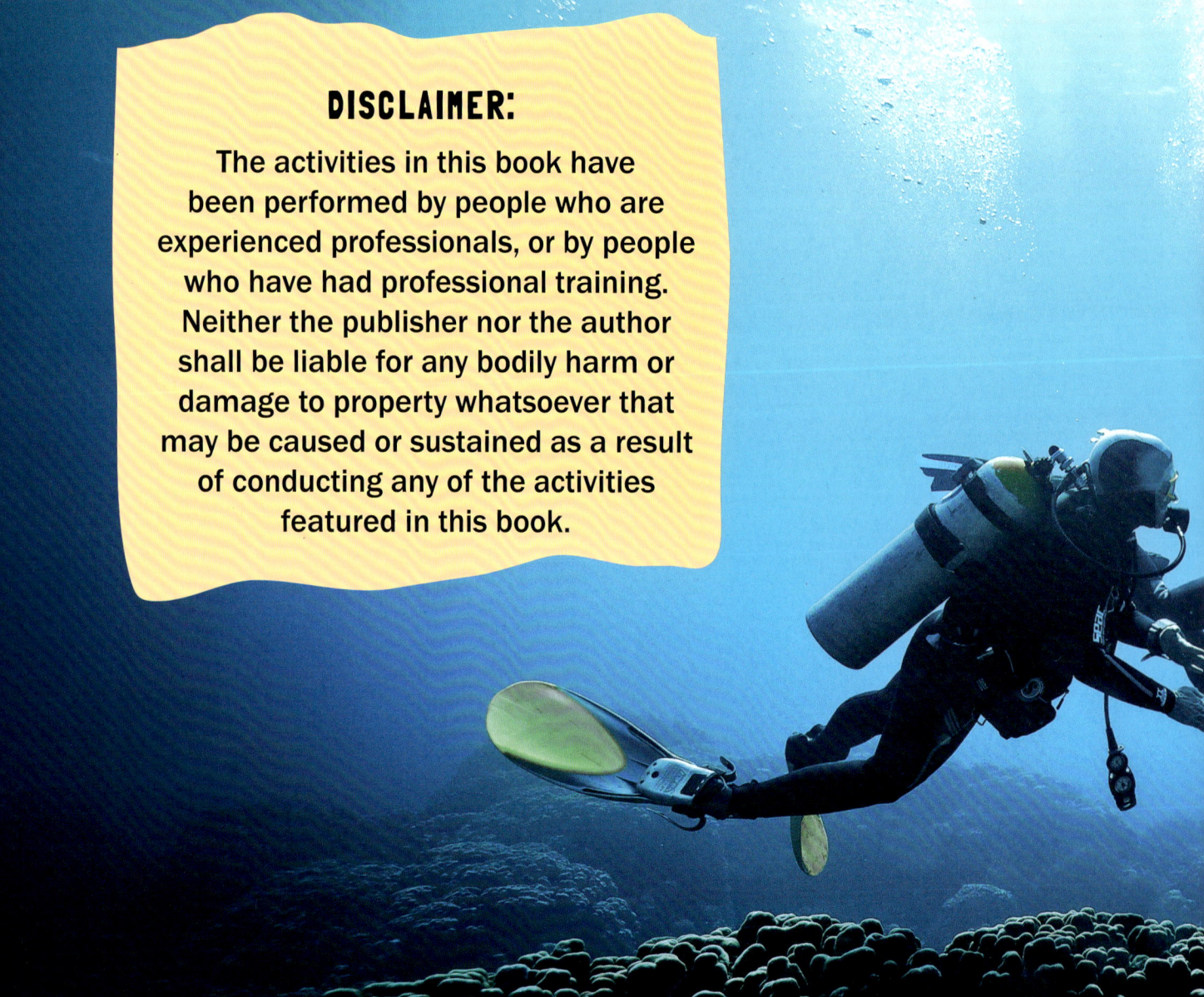

DISCLAIMER:

The activities in this book have been performed by people who are experienced professionals, or by people who have had professional training. Neither the publisher nor the author shall be liable for any bodily harm or damage to property whatsoever that may be caused or sustained as a result of conducting any of the activities featured in this book.

Words in **BOLD** can be found in the glossary.

DEEP SEA DIVING	20	RECORD BREAKERS	28
INTO THE UNKNOWN	22	GLOSSARY	30
ICE DIVING	24	INDEX	31
FREE DIVING	26		

INTRODUCTION TO DIVING

There are millions of divers in the world. They dive into a world of coral reefs, underwater forests, and ice caves. Some divers swim freely, and others use **watercraft** to explore the mysteries of the deep.

THE DANGEROUS DEEP

Divers have to stay alert when exploring the world's oceans. Not only do they have to keep an eye on their equipment to make sure they have enough **oxygen**, and aren't deeper than it is safe to be, they must always stay aware of their surroundings.

The oceans are wild places, full of animals that may feel confused or threatened by humans. Divers must keep their distance and avoid **provoking** ocean animals while in their territory.

DID YOU KNOW?

The ocean covers 70% of the Earth's surface and holds about 97% of Earth's water. The ocean is so vast that scientists think they've only discovered a tiny number of the plant and animal **species** that live there!

TYPES OF DIVING

There are many different types of diving!

CLIFF DIVING

CAGE DIVING

SCUBA DIVING

DEEP SEA DIVING

ICE DIVING

FREE DIVING

CLIFF DIVING

Cliff divers take off from heights of 20 to 35 metres (65-115 ft). Each dive usually only lasts for about 3 seconds! The divers spin and twist in the air, then hit the water at over 60 miles per hour (100 km/h).

SAFE LANDING

Unlike high divers who dive into swimming pools headfirst, cliff divers land in the ocean feetfirst. This is to reduce the risk of head and neck injury. When moving at such incredible speeds, even hitting something small, like a piece of seaweed, can leave a diver with a broken foot!

TOP SPOT

There are many cliff diving spots around the world, but the sport first started on the Hawaiian island of Lanai. Nearly 250 years ago, warriors jumped off cliffs into the ocean to show their bravery. The same site is sometimes used for cliff diving world championships today.

DID YOU KNOW?

Cliff divers don't just dive into the ocean! Some jump into freshwater lakes. The main thing they look for are **rocky outcrops** above deep water.

TRUE STORY

After jumping from a 32 metres (106 ft) cliff and landing flat on his back in 2024, stuntman Kevin Kahwaty suffered an "exploded lung" and a cut behind his ear so deep that it nearly came off!

NO PLACE FOR FEAR

Cliff diving can be an incredibly dangerous sport, so divers must make sure they are well prepared. Professional cliff divers always take care to plan ahead before making their jumps.

THE DIVE ZONE

The dive zone is the area of water where the divers must land. It has to be chosen carefully to make sure the water is deep enough, and that there are no dangers, like rocks or strong **currents**, nearby. In competitions, the safety crew splash near the dive zone to help the diver see the water's surface. They are on stand-by in case something goes wrong.

PREPARATION IS KEY

Divers must do warm-up exercises for their legs, arms, and backs before jumping. During competitions, teams of **physiotherapists** help athletes prepare their bodies. It's not just physical strength, mental strength is also key – athletes must focus their minds before they dive.

Lots of people are around to help divers stay safe in big competitions.

Both men and women compete in the Cliff Diving World Series.

TRUE STORY

In 2017, American diver Steven LoBue became the first person to do five somersaults in a three-second freefall! It won him gold in the FINA World Championships.

CAGE DIVING

The thrill of cage diving is seeing great white sharks close up. Divers watch the sharks through the bars of a metal cage. Cage diving is all about seeing the sharks swimming free in their natural **habitat**.

BEST DIVES

Cage diving trips are run by expert teams. Some of the best dive sites in the world are in the ocean waters off California (USA), Mexico, South Africa, and Australia.

BLOOD IN THE WATER

To attract the sharks, the boat crew sometimes throw chum into the water. Chum is made of chunks of fish meat, bones, and blood. When the sharks appear, the divers climb into the cage, the lid is shut tight, and the cage is lowered into the water. The cage is tied to the boat but floats a short distance away.

DID YOU KNOW?

Some people say that throwing chum into the water is **unethical** as it draws the sharks away from where they were on a false-promise of food. It is banned in some places for this reason.

TRUE STORY

Cage diving isn't just done by tourists wanting to see these powerful animals up close, it's often done by scientists to observe animals too.

UP CLOSE AND PERSONAL

Most diving cages are small, but very strong. The bars can stand the fury of a shark attack, although these are rare. Divers wear wetsuits, boots, and a mask. They also wear a weight belt which helps them to balance underwater. Some use breathing aparatus so they can stay underwater for a while.

INSIDE THE CAGE

Divers must stay still inside the diving cage. Great whites swim right up to the bars. Some people want to feel the shark's skin, but it's strictly forbidden. Cage diving isn't about interacting with sharks, it's about observing and respecting them.

DIVING DEEP?

Different companies use different types of cages. Surface cages are completely open at the top because that part is kept above the water. Divers hold their breath while underwater and swim up for air or use a snorkel. Some cages are submerged around 5 to 10 metres (16-33 ft). Divers in these cages wear scuba gear to breathe underwater.

DID YOU KNOW?

Although some sharks can be dangerous to humans, there are less than 10 deaths a year from shark attacks. But every year, humans kill 100 million sharks. Today, more than one third of shark species are threatened with extinction.

SCUBA DIVING

Divers that want to stay underwater for a long time need to carry their own air supply with them so that they can keep breathing! These divers are called scuba divers. The air comes from a cylinder on their back.

FIRST LESSONS

Scuba diving courses can be completed from the age of 10. These start with confined water dives to learn basic skills, before progressing to open water dives, when divers can gain junior certification.

SCUBA TANK AND REGULARTOR
The tank holds the diver's air. It's connected to the regulator, which is the mouthpiece divers breathe from.

FINS
Fins make swimming easier as they push divers through the water more quickly than their feet can.

BUOYANCY CONTROL DEVICE
This is a jacket that goes over the wetsuit. Divers can pump or release air from the jacket to go higher or lower in the water.

BUDDY SYSTEM

For safety reasons, scuba divers rarely dive alone. They use a buddy system where divers look out for each other. Communication is done by special hand signals. This diver is using the signal that they are "OK".

MASK
Scuba masks are bigger than swimming goggles – they cover the eyes and nose!

DIVE COMPUTER
This device shows all sorts of stats, including the depth, time, water pressure, and how much air you have left.

SCUBA SIGHTS

How deep divers can go depends on the level they're certified to dive at. But divers don't have to be deep to see amazing sights. There are many fantastic shallow scuba diving sites to explore around the world.

UNDERWATER TREASURE HUNT

The Great Barrier Reef in Australia is one of the world's top scuba diving destinations. It's the biggest coral reef, and is filled with thousands of types of coral, seaweed, fish, and other ocean creatures. The water here is crystal clear, perfect for seeing the sights.

SPOOKY WRECKS

Shipwrecks are another really popular type of dive site to visit. The SS Thistlegorm wreck off the coast of Egypt is one of the most famous. Here, divers can step into the past and look at the trunks, motorcycles, and tanks that the boat was carrying when it sank in 1941.

TRUE STORY

In 1998, two American scuba divers went missing in the seas of the Great Barrier Reef. A tourist dive boat left them behind by mistake, and their bodies were never found.

BLUE HOLES

Blue holes are some of the most curious things divers have discovered. These deep, dark areas of the ocean are incredibly dangerous places to dive! The divers who brave them and make it back to the surface have amazing stories. But not everyone is so lucky...

SECRETS OF THE DEEP

Blue holes are **sinkholes** that form when the rocky ocean floor collapses to reveal underwater caves. Many have tunnels inside too. Blue holes haven't been fully explored, so there's still lots to learn, but they're thought to be full of unusual plants and animals.

DANGEROUS TERRITORY

Only experienced divers are allowed to explore blue holes. Divers must always go with a trained guide, never alone. Divers often carry double air tanks and are sometimes linked together by safety ropes. Some choose to wear extra thick wetsuits to combat the cold water.

DID YOU KNOW?

The Giant Blue Hole in Belize is the biggest of all. As it's full of **stalactites**, scientists think that thousands of years ago, the sea level was lower, and this cave was on land. Over time, the ocean has risen and covered it.

TRUE STORY

In the Bahamas, local legends tell of the lusca who live in blue holes. Described as giant sea monsters, the lusca is blamed for the disappearance of divers who explore blue holes.

DEEP SEA DIVING

Most scuba diving takes place in shallow water up to 30 metres (98 ft) deep. As 90% of the world's oceans are more than 1 kilometre (3,280 ft) deep, there are huge areas of ocean floor we know nothing about. Deep sea divers plan to change that.

DID YOU KNOW?

Divers who return to the surface too quickly can get decompression sickness, which is also called "the bends". It causes body pains, dizzy spells, and sickness. If left untreated, it can cause permanent damage.

DEEP SEA DANGER

Professional scuba divers dive up to 40 metres (130 ft) deep, but deep-sea divers go further. But diving deeper is dangerous – the deeper you go, the higher the water pressure gets. Under pressure, gases in the air tank can change, causing divers to become confused and make unsafe decisions.

OUT OF THIS WORLD

Atmospheric diving suits can reduce the effects of high pressure, letting divers go deeper and stay longer. With domed helmets, bendy metal arms, and **thrusters**, they look like space suits! Designs are improving all the time.

TRUE STORY

The deepest human dive ever was done in a **submersible**. In 2019, explorer Victor Vesco reached the deepest discovered point in our oceans – 10,927 metres (35,852 ft) down – at **Challenger Deep**. This record may never be broken.

INTO THE UNKNOWN

No light reaches the deepest parts of the ocean, but strange creatures make their homes in the dark waters. It's a creepy, mysterious world that we have only just begun exploring.

IN DEEP WATER

Scientists divide the ocean into layers based on how far light reaches. Different creatures have **adapted** to live in each layer. The deepest layer is the trenches, which are 6 to 7 miles (10-11 km) down. That deep, it's pitch black and freezing cold!

MAKING WAVES

The first crewed dive to the deepest trenches was in 1960 by Don Walsh and Jacques Piccard in the submersible, Trieste. People thought that nothing lived that deep, but the explorers saw fish. Since then, many deep-sea creatures have been discovered on both crewed and uncrewed missions.

CREATURES OF THE DEEP

Here's a small selection of the weird and wonderful deep-sea animals that have been discovered.

BRIGHT LIGHTS

Deep-sea creatures have learnt to create their own light. Anglerfish have a light on the end of their forehead, which they use to attract and catch their **prey**!

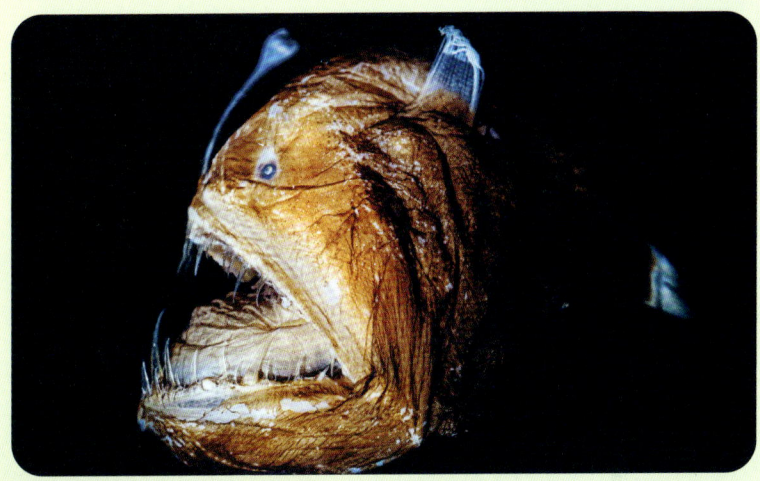

HAPPY WITHOUT FOOD

Food can be hard to come by on the ocean floor. That's not a problem for giant tube worms – they don't eat, instead they transform chemicals in the water into energy to stay alive.

GIANTS OF ALL KINDS

Giant squid are rare animals. They don't live the deepest of all, but they are still like something from a nightmare. They grow to be 13 metres (43 ft) long – almost as long as a bowling lane!

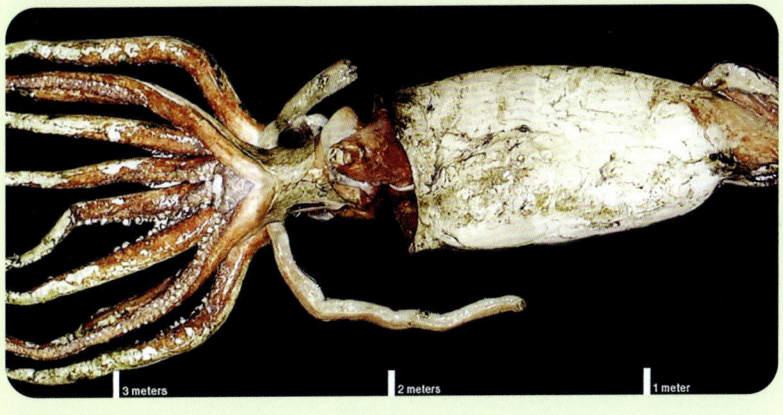

ICE DIVING

Divers must always take care to stay warm, especially when exploring under ice! Instead of wetsuits, ice divers wear drysuits, which don't let any water in and have room underneath for an **undersuit**. They also wear hoods, gloves, and full-face masks.

HARD TRUTH

A lot of ice diving takes place in frozen lakes, and often divers have to cut a hole in the ice, using a pickaxe or chainsaw, to reach the water! They enter the water through the hole, and swim under the ice.

TIED TO THE SURFACE

Ice dives usually only last 20 to 30 minutes – any longer increases risk of **hypothermia**. Divers are tied to a rope, and use rope signals so that they can be pulled back to the surface hole if they get in trouble. A rescue diver is always ready to jump in and help if needed.

DID YOU KNOW?

Ice divers in Canada's Arctic Bay have a good chance of seeing polar bears. Over half of the world's polar bears live in Canada!

FREE DIVING

Not all diving requires lots of equipment – in free diving, divers hold their breath while underwater! This is a true test of mental and physical strength. It can take years of training to increase the amount of time they can hold their breath for.

TIMELESS CHALLENGE

While most types of diving in this book are modern, free diving is ancient – humans have been free diving to reach food, or collect goods to sell, for at least 8,000 years! Today, there are many extra reasons to free dive: some people do it for fun or to challenge themselves; others compete on a global scale.

TECHNIQUES FOR SUCCESS

Free diving isn't just swimming underwater – it requires training. Free divers need to learn how to improve their breath-hold, **equalise** their ears to avoid injury, and streamline themselves to help save energy during a dive.

DID YOU KNOW?

One of the most important things for free divers is to listen to their bodies and not push too hard.

TRUE STORY

Free divers improve their breath-hold by staying still underwater in a swimming pool. The longest static breath-hold was 24 minutes and 37 seconds, achieved by Budimir Šobat in 2021.

RECORD BREAKERS

The history books of diving are filled with amazing record breakers. Here are just a few of the brave people who have done impressive things and changed the way people think about diving.

LONGEST SALTWATER SCUBA DIVE

In 2020, Saddam Killany set an incredible record by completing the world's longest open saltwater scuba dive. His dive lasted 145 hours, 25 minutes, and 25 seconds – that's 6 days!

DEEPEST SCUBA DIVE

Ahmed Gabr holds the record for the deepest scuba dive, with a depth of 332 metres (1,090 ft). It took him about 12 minutes to reach that depth, but 15 hours to come back to the surface slowly.

FIRST ICEBERG DIVE

Cave diving explorer, Jill Heinerth, led the first ice dive inside an iceberg! They almost got trapped when huge chunks of ice shifted, but thankfully made it safely out.

HIGHEST CLIFF DIVE

The world record for the highest cliff dive is held by Laso Schaller, who jumped from a 58.5-metre (192-ft) high waterfall in Switzerland into the water below.

WHAT IT TAKES TO BE THE BEST

It takes lots of mental and physical strength, training time, and dedication to break a world record in diving. Depending on the type of record, people don't always break it on their first attempt. Once the record is broken, they also have to hold onto it! This means defending your record if someone else breaks it.

GLOSSARY

Adapted – when a living thing has developed special features or skills to help it survive in its environment.

Challenger Deep – the deepest known point on Earth. It's located in the Mariana Trench in the Pacific Ocean.

Currents – powerful movement of water from one place to another.

Equalise ears – to re-balance the pressure in your ears, which builds and causes pain as you dive deeper.

Habitat – the place(s) where animals and plants naturally live.

Hypothermia – a condition when the human body drops to a worryingly low temperature.

Oxygen – an invisible gas in the air that plants produce, and people and animals need to breathe.

Physiotherapists – people who are trained to help others move their body correctly, including increasing flexibility and reducing pain.

Prey – an animal that is hunted by other animals for food.

Provoking – encouraging someone or something to react to you.

Rocky outcrops – large structures made of exposed rock.

Sinkholes – large holes in the ground caused by collapse of the surface. These can form in the ocean or on land.

Species – a group of living things that share characteristics and features.

Stalactites – formations that are made from minerals, but that look like icicles and grow down from cave ceilings.

Submersible – a small watercraft that is designed for research and exploration. Submersibles can be controlled remotely or have a crew.

Thrusters – parts of a machine that create a forward motion, and help people move in air or water.

Undersuit – usually an all-in-one piece of clothing that fits under a drysuit to keep a diver extra warm.

Unethical – wrong or unacceptable.

Watercraft – any vehicle designed for travel across, or through, water.

INDEX

A
Animals 4, 10-11, 12-13, 15, 16, 18, 23, 25
Arctic Bay, Canada 25
Atmospheric diving suits 21

B
Blue holes 18-19

C
Cage diving 5, 10-11, 12-13
Challenger Deep, Pacific Ocean 21, 30
Cliff diving 5, 6-7, 8-9, 28

D
Decompression sickness 20
Deep sea diving 5, 20-21
Drysuits 24

E
Extinction 13

F
Free diving 5, 26-27

G
Gabr, Ahmed 28
Giant Blue Hole, Belize 19
Great Barrier Reef 16-17

H
Heinerth, Jill 28
High diving 6

I
Ice diving 5, 24-25, 28

K
Kahwaty, Kevin 7
Killany, Saddam 28

L
Lanai, Hawaii 6
LoBue, Steven 9
Lusca 19

P
Piccard, Jacques 22
Plants 4, 18

S
Schaller, Laso 28
Scuba diving 5, 14-15, 16-17, 20-21, 28
Scuba gear 13, 14-15
Šobat, Budimir 27
SS Thistlegorm, Egypt 17

T
The bends (see: *Decompression sickness*)
Training 14, 16, 21, 26-27, 29
True stories 7, 9, 11, 17, 19, 21, 27, 28

U
Undersuits 24, 30

V
Vesco, Victor 21

W
Walsh, Don 22
Wetsuits 12, 14, 19
World championships 6, 9
Word records 21, 28-29

Copyright © 2025 Hungry Tomato Ltd

First published in 2025 by Hungry Tomato Ltd
F15, Old Bakery Studios, Blewetts Wharf, Malpas Road, Truro, Cornwall,
TR1 1QH, UK.

No part of this publication may be reproduced, stored in a retrieval system, or transmitted in any form or by any means, electronic, mechanical, photocopying, recording, or otherwise, without prior written permission of the copyright owner.

A CIP catalogue record for this book is available from the British Library.

ISBN 9781835694305

Printed in China

Discover more at
www.hungrytomato.com

Picture Credits
(abbreviations: t = top; b = bottom; m = middle; l = left; r = right; bg = background)

Wikipedia: Clemens Vasters (IMG_4970_edited-1.jpg) 21mr; Flickr NOAA Photo Library 23ml; NH 96801 U.S. Navy Bathyscaphe Trieste (1958-1963) 22br. NASA/Wikipedia: 23br. Shutterstock: Brandelet 13br; Damsea 22m; Dmitry Pradun 10-11bg; Dudarev Mikhail FC, 27bg; Flystock 5tl; JamiesOnAMission 18m; Janik Rybicka 24m; Jessica Seghatti 13m; Juergen Nowak 9bg; Kondratuk Aleksei 5bm; lauraslens 6-7bg; Ljupco Smokovski 32b; Lillac 20-21bg; Lucia.Pinto 1bg, 14-15bg; MuhammadHanif1 25br; paul saad 8b; nartt 5br; Shane Myers Photography 11tr, 12m; silvae 4br; Stefan Pircher 5tm; Sun_Shine 2-3bg; Sven Hansche 5bl; Tuulia Ristola 6br; Rich Carey 5tr, 16-17bg, 17tr, 19t; Ryan Sleiman 28-29bg; Wonderful Nature 26m.

Every effort has been made to trace the copyright holders and we apologise in advance for any unintentional omissions. We would be pleased to insert the appropriate credit in any subsequent edition of this publication.